MOTOCROSS

By Anthony Sutton

CAPSTONE PRESS
a capstone imprint

Velocity is published by
Capstone Press, a Capstone imprint,
151 Good Counsel Drive, P.O. Box 669,
Mankato, Minnesota 56002.

www.capstonepub.com

052011
006207ACF11

WARNING!
**Motocross training is dangerous and must
be undertaken only under the supervision
of a trained instructor. Readers should
never attempt to undertake the
techniques described in this book without
the supervision of such an instructor.**

**Always wear complete safety gear while
riding, including a helmet, chest protector,
boots, and pads.**

The authors and publishers of this book
assume no legal or financial responsibility,
either direct or implied, that may result
from the use, abuse, or misuse of the
information contained herein.

The right of Anthony Sutton to be identified as
the author of this work has been asserted by
him in accordance with the Copyright, Designs
and Patents Act 1988.

Library of Congress Cataloging-in-Publication
Data
Sutton, Anthony.
    Motocross : how to be an awesome
motocross rider / by Anthony Sutton.
        p. cm. -- (Velocity. instant expert.)
    Includes bibliographical references and
    index.
    Summary: "Describes the sport of
motocross, giving tips on race preparation,
choosing equipment, racing techniques, dirt
bike maintenance, and other information for
how to become a skilled motocross rider"--
Provided by publisher.
    ISBN 978-1-4296-6886-6 (hardcover)
    1. Motocross--Juvenile literature. I. Title. II.
Series.
    GV1060.12.S88 2012
    796.7'56--dc23
2011020146

Photo acknowledgements:
All interior photos © Anthony Sutton
Cover: Main image © Alain Cimon
Photography, all others Shutterstock

First published 2011
Copyright © 2011 A & C Black
Publishers Limited

Original concept: Paul Mason
Project management: Paul Mason
Design: Mayer Media

Contents

Why become a motocross expert?

Get the low-down on becoming a motocross (MX) expert and you'll be on the fast track to being a better, safer and faster racer. You'll be ready to handle anything the weather, the track or the competition throws at you. You'll also know where to ride, the safety equipment you need and much more.

HELP YOUR FRIENDS

Tune up your motocross skills by reading this book, and you'll be passing your friends on the track before you know it. Of course, you'll probably want to share with them the tricks and tips you've learned.

FYI!

These features are scattered throughout the book. They contain information you can casually drop into conversation to amaze, astound, and impress your friends.

The secrets of motocross can be yours. All you have to do is read on!

SAVE CASH

Crashing costs money in broken parts. By becoming a motocross expert, you're bound to save cash. Who knows, maybe one day you might also win some prize money!

FINDING THE RIGHT INFO

At the back of the book there's a troubleshooting section that'll help you figure out what's going wrong with your riding. Maybe you are:

- Nosediving over jumps?

- Slipping off in turns?

- Falling behind at the start?

For these and other common problems, troubleshooting tells you where to look for the fix. Or if you know exactly what the problem is, just use the contents page or index to go straight to the relevant place.

REMEMBER!

These panels tell you one thing you should always try to remember.

LOST FOR WORDS

Look here for explanations of those tricky, technical words.

Motocross bikes

When motocross began, the bikes were stripped-down road machines with knobby tires and race numbers painted on. Today, they're highly specialized race-bred rockets. Aside from having two wheels, an engine and some handlebars, today's bikes bear little resemblance to street motorcycles. So what makes motocross bikes unique?

! There are two key classes in MX racing in the United States:
• **The 450 Class is for 150-250cc two-stroke and 251-450cc four-stroke motorcycles.**
• **The 250 Class is for two-stroke motorcycles up to 125cc and 150-250cc four-strokes.**

Race numbers on and fully prepared, this motocross bike is ready to hit the track.

ENGINES

Motocross engines have to deliver a wide spread of power with instant throttle response so that the rider can accelerate very quickly. Most bikes use highly tuned **four-stroke** engines. A few use **two-stroke** engines instead. Two-strokes normally race against four-strokes that are twice as big, because they are roughly twice as efficient as four-strokes. For example, 125cc two-strokes race 250cc four-strokes.

SUSPENSION

With up to 13 in (330 mm) of suspension travel in the front and rear, motocross bikes are able to soak up bumps and jumps with ease. The front forks and rear suspension can be tuned to suit an individual rider's weight, speed or riding style.

four-stroke engine that produces power every two turns of the crankshaft
two-stroke engine that produces power on each turn of the crankshaft

SECRET TRICK

How can you spot if a bike has a two-stroke or four-stroke motor? The easiest way is to check the size and shape of its exhaust pipe.

1 All two-stroke machines have bulging sections of pipe leading from the engine to the silencer. This bulge in the exhaust helps increase engine power.

BRAKES

Powerful hydraulic disc brakes are fitted to both wheels of the bike, but it's the front brake that does the majority of the work when slowing the machine down. The steel discs are drilled or slotted to aid cooling and to clear dirt from the braking surface. The pads are designed to be durable with a powerful grip.

TIRES

With their deep tread patterns, motocross tires can really grip into the dirt. They offer the rider good grip in almost all conditions. Motocross tires come in compounds and tread patterns designed to suit anything from baked-hard clay to super-slippery mud.

FYI!

Before 1980 all motocross bikes came with two shock absorbers on the rear instead of just one like we see today. This type of bike is now commonly known as a twin-shock.

2 The front section of a four-stroke exhaust pipe is the same width all the way. The silencer has to be much bigger compared to a two-stroke machine's to deaden the extra exhaust noise a four-stroke motor makes.

Ken Roczen

Even when he had only just become a teenager Ken Roczen was already one of the world's most expert motocross riders. At 13, Roczen was junior world champion in the 85cc division, and was all set to become the next big star in the MX2 world championship.

STARTING YOUNG

Born in Germany, Roczen started racing at the age of three. It soon became apparent that he was an extremely talented rider, and Roczen sped through the **amateur** ranks. In 2007 he won the 85cc Junior World Championship. In 2008 Roczen raced on full-size bikes as an amateur, but achieved little in the way of major championship success. He did, though, race well at Loretta Lynn's – the United States' biggest and most important amateur motocross event.

SUCCESS AS A PRO

Roczen turned **pro** for the 2009 season. At 14, he was too young to enter the first four rounds of the 2009 world championship. As soon as his 15th birthday came around, though, Roczen was ready to race. At his home race at the German circuit of Teutschenthal, he came in second in both **motos** and took the first overall win of his Grand Prix (GP) career. Roczen also became the youngest-ever GP winner, at just 15 years and 53 days old. More GP victories followed in 2010, although a string of mechanical failures meant he had to be content with the runner-up spot in the final world championship points table.

amateur person who does an activity without pay

moto single round of a motocross event

pro professional, a person paid to do an activity

2011 AND ONWARD

In 2011 Roczen signed to race for Red Bull-KTM, which is among the world's strongest MX teams. Whatever success follows Roczen's move, this hard-working teenage sensation is a great example for all would-be motocross racers to follow.

FACT FILE

Name: Ken Roczen

Date of birth: 4/28/94

Nationality: German

Height: 5' 6" (170 cm)

Weight: 132 pounds (60 kg)

Residence: Mattstedt, Germany

Marital status: Single

Favorite music: Punk, Limp Bizkit, Linkin Park

Favorite food: Pizza

Favorite drink: Red Bull

Hobbies: Snowboarding

Ken's advice to young motocross riders is simple. Don't practice or train too much at a really young age – just enjoy riding. He says you only understand the things you need to train harder at once you get a bit older.

FYI!

Ken's favorite pet is a huge German Mastiff dog called Blacky.

Buying a used bike

Motocross bikes live a hard life. When buying a used bike, look at its general condition and try to figure out if it's been looked after. Don't be blinded by sticker kits or cool-looking parts. If the bike looks unloved, don't buy it, however cheap it seems. So which parts should you check before buying?

> **!**
>
> If you remember one thing about buying a used bike, make it:
> • **Check the engine and frame numbers first,** (see the Secret Trick on page 11) then the condition of the bike.

This used bike looks great – but you'd need to give it a careful check-over before parting with any cash.

SPROCKETS

Look for worn or damaged **sprockets**. If the sprocket is bent or the teeth are worn unevenly so that they look like little shark fins, the sprocket and chain *both* need to be replaced.

AIRBOX

Ask the seller to take off the seat or remove the cover to let you look inside the airbox. (If they don't know how, don't buy the bike.) This area of the bike should always be spotless and the air filter should be clean and freshly oiled.

BRAKES

The braking surface of the disc should be flat and have no grooves in it. The brake pads should have at least 3 mm of material left on them. Pads and discs are not too expensive or difficult to replace, but do negotiate a discount on the price if they are worn.

sprocket toothed disc on the rear wheel, which connects to the chain

ENGINE AND GEARBOX
Visually check the engine for any damage or oil leaks. Next, start it up and listen for any unusual noises or knocking, while feeling for heavy vibration. Put the bike on a stand so the rear wheel is off the ground, and run through the gears. Make sure you can select all the gears and that there are no nasty noises coming from the transmission.

SUSPENSION
Check for fluid leaks from the forks and rear suspension, then push down on the bike to compress them. Unusual noises or a clunky feel mean big repair bills are likely to be coming up soon.

FYI!
At least three manufacturers are currently developing electric-powered motocross bikes.

SECRET TRICK
It's important to check the bike you are buying isn't stolen. Buying a stolen bike can lead to you having to hand it back to the original owner, or even being prosecuted by the police.

1 Most importantly, check the engine (a) and frame (b) numbers. If they've been removed or tampered with, don't buy the bike.

2 Try to get some proof that the seller does really own the bike, as well as evidence of where he or she lives.

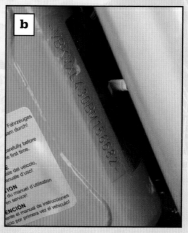

3 Ask the owner if he or she has a service book for the bike or receipts for work that has been done on it.

Riding **equipment**

! If you remember one thing about buying riding equipment, make it:
- **Always try it on! Sizing differs from brand to brand.**

Racing associations require that riders wear certain safety equipment. Other pieces of equipment are optional but equally important. Here's everything you need to know about protecting yourself while you're behind the handlebars.

HELMET AND GOGGLES

Brain injuries are extremely serious, so always protect your head with the best-quality, best-fitting helmet you can afford. Eye injuries can also be serious and permanent, so every time you hit the track make sure you are wearing good-quality goggles. When buying goggles, make sure they fit inside the eye port of your helmet and that the foam seals against your face all the way around.

BOOTS

Only buy specialty MX boots. Try on as many different pairs as you can and buy the ones that fit best. Ideally you're looking for some that hold your ankles snugly, but that aren't so stiff that you struggle to move your ankles. If the boots are too stiff you will find it tricky to change gears or use the rear brake.

roost dirt, dust and debris thrown up by the wheels of a motocross bike

To protect your head properly a helmet needs to fit perfectly. When putting on a helmet, take hold of the two chinstraps, pull on the straps, and then pull the helmet over your head.

1 When the helmet's in place your eyes should be in the center of the eye port. The padding should be in contact with your head, forehead, and cheeks, but not so tight that it pinches.

PROTECTION
Body armor can protect your upper body, joints and limbs in crashes, as well as take the sting out of flying **roost**. The ideal armor offers maximum protection but doesn't make it hard to move around on the bike. Your knees also need protection every time you ride. Many riders use knee braces, but these can be expensive. Those who can't afford knee braces get kneepads instead.

2 To check for correct fit, get someone to try and move the helmet on your head. Rather than rolling around loosely on your head, the helmet should move only as much as your skin will let it.

FYI!
Fifty years ago, 'safety gear' was comprised of leather trousers, rugby shirts and military-style helmets.

Where to ride

! If you remember one thing about riding off-road, make it:
• **Get permission to ride before starting your bike.**

You've got a bike and all the gear – now it's time to get out and do some riding! Where can you go to practice? This section will clue you into where and where not to ride, plus give you some tips on the best time to go riding.

FYI!

In some countries, riding in places illegally can lead to your bike being taken and destroyed.

Finding a practice track shouldn't be too tricky.

This landowner has made his or her feelings about off-road riders pretty clear.

WHERE NOT TO RIDE

In general it's safe to assume that you *can't* ride on a piece of land unless you have permission from the landowner or leaseholder. Public land, parks, beaches, footpaths, fields and trails are also **off limits**. So are recognized racetracks, unless there's a race or an official practice session going on and you have permission to take part.

 off limits not available for use

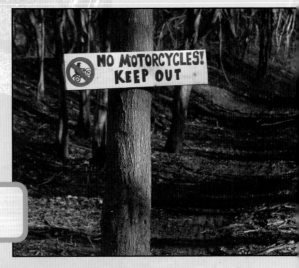

FINDING A PRACTICE TRACK

The biggest and best tracks will be advertised. Check magazines and scour the Internet for information. If that doesn't give you some ideas for tracks in the area that you could use, try asking your local dirt-bike dealer and other riders where they go.

GOING RACING

Most riders will find that there are at least a couple of races in their local area. It's usually best to start off at these small, local races. If you improve enough to start winning local races, it's time to look for harder challenges.

SECRET TRICK

When to go riding can be as important as where you go riding. This decision depends on your level of skill and what you want to get out of your practice or training session.

1 If you're still new to MX, the morning might be the best time. You'll benefit from riding a freshly prepared track, which will be smoother, safer and much less demanding to ride. You'll be able to concentrate on applying good riding techniques rather than battling the track.

2 If you're already a skilled rider, wait until later in the day to go riding. The track will be much rougher and will offer you more of a physical challenge as you pound out your practice runs.

15

Fitness and training

Motocross is one of the most physically demanding sports there is. To get the most enjoyment out of a day at the races, you need to be in good shape. These tips will help keep training fun.

! If you remember one thing about training, make it:
• **Always do a form of physical exercise you enjoy.**

Mountain biking is excellent cross-training for motocross riding.

HAVING FUN
The best training for MX is riding, but many people like to combine that with other activities. The key to good training is finding something that's physically demanding but still fun. You could try these for starters:

• Running is great for improving **aerobic** fitness, though it is relatively hard on the knees and ankles.

• Cycling and swimming are good activities for riders who have existing knee or ankle injuries.

• Mountain biking offers a similar thrill to MX, and uses many of the same muscle groups.

• Skateboarding, snowboarding and surfing all build fitness and are good training for your legs.

INJURIES
Motocross is a tough sport and it's not uncommon for a rider to get injured. If that happens to you, don't put a total stop to your training. Try instead to work around the injury. For instance, if you have an upper-body injury, try cycling on a static bike.

FYI!
Scientific tests have proven that professional motocross racers are among the fittest athletes in the world.

FUELING THE BODY

Good diet is really important if you want to perform properly on race day. If you're training hard and racing regularly, you will need a diet that includes protein, **complex carbohydrates**, calcium, vitamins and iron.

WATER IS BETTER

If you start to **dehydrate**, your strength, endurance and speed of movement will all be affected. Most people need to drink around 2 liters (4.2 pints) of water a day to stay in peak condition. If you're training and racing hard you'll need more than this.

aerobic with oxygen; aerobic exercise improves the performance of the heart and lungs, which circulate oxygen to the muscles
complex carbohydrate a food that provides energy and helps digestion, such as brown rice, spinach and potatoes
dehydrate lose fluid from the body

STICK TO IT

The benefits of physical training take a while to become evident. When you've started training, stick to it. You'll be glad you did when the wins start rolling in!

Accelerating

Proper acceleration is one of the most overlooked skills in motocross. Learning to accelerate well is *guaranteed* to lower your lap times. There's a lot more to it than just opening the throttle as wide as possible! Body position and clutch control are equally important.

! If you remember one thing about accelerating, make it:
- **Be sure you're in the correct position on the bike *before* you open the throttle.**

THE BASICS

Whether you're opening the throttle after coming out of a corner or landing from a jump, get your body position correctly balanced before accelerating. If you're too far forward the rear wheel is likely to lose grip. If you're too far back your bike may get too much grip and could **loop out**. It's important to stay central on the bike at all times so that you're ready to make quick adjustments when necessary.

THE ATTACK POSITION

Whether sitting or standing there are certain body-position guidelines you should follow that will help you maximize bike control. Look forward toward upcoming obstacles. Your elbows should be high and your knees should be bent – but still carrying your weight – and your back should be arched slightly forward. This is known as the **attack position**.

CLUTCH CONTROL

Whenever you are riding you should have one or two fingers covering the clutch lever. This is particularly important when accelerating. You can pull in the clutch slightly to get the engine up to speed if it is struggling in too high a gear. Similarly if your front wheel lifts because you have too much traction you can momentarily pull in the clutch to regain control.

attack position optimum riding position when accelerating or approaching obstacles
loop out crash caused when the front wheel comes up so high that the rider falls off the back of the bike
throttle twist grip on right side of handlebar that controls a motorcycle's acceleration

SECRET TRICK

How do you keep your right elbow high, in the attack position, when you're opening the throttle all the way? The secret is to use the over-grip procedure.

1 To pull the over-grip off like a pro you need to rotate your wrist away from your body and grip the throttle in an exaggerated off position.

2 If you start in this position, when you twist the throttle backward to accelerate, your wrist will be in line with your arm. This gives maximum control.

FYI!

Motocross bikes are geared to accelerate quickly from corner to corner, rather than for a high top speed.

19

Braking

!

If you remember one thing about braking, make it:

- **Once your body is in the correct position, apply the brakes progressively.**

The quicker you can ride your bike in a straight line the better you'll need to be at braking – unless you like going straight ahead at turns! These top tips will have you slowing down your dirt bike quicker and more safely than ever before.

THE BASICS

Slowing down your motocross bike safely means much more than simply applying both brakes. As with all other riding skills, having the correct body position is vital. For braking, the stance you need to adopt is similar to the standard attack position. Just lean a little farther back to move your weight toward the rear of the bike. This will balance the bike and keep the rear wheel planted on the ground.

USING THE BRAKES

Your front brake does most of the work of slowing your bike. The rear brake also plays an important part, however. It keeps the bike in a straight line and stops the rear wheel from lifting off the ground. When applying the brakes, do it progressively, rather than braking hard immediately. Avoid **locking up** the front wheel, and if the front wheel does start to skid, release the brake momentarily while you regain control.

SECRET TRICK

You'd be surprised how many racers have their front brake lever set up so it's more tiring and difficult to use than it needs to be. This leads to the rider relying on the less effective rear brake late in the moto as his or her arms tire.

1 Slacken the lever off on the adjuster. This will cause the brake to work much closer to the handlebar grip than it did previously.

PICK THE RIGHT LINE

While trying to position yourself on the track for an obstacle or turn, try and choose a **line** that avoids slick spots, stones, or anything else that could cause the tires to slip. If they do slip, it will have a negative effect on your bike's ability to slow down safely and effectively.

line specific route or direction of travel followed by a bike
locking up skidding

2 Make sure that your fingers do not have to bend downward or upward to grip the brake lever. It (and the clutch lever) should be in line with your forearm. If they are not, get an expert mechanic to adjust them for you.

These adjustments will give you more control over the machine and put less strain on your hand and forearm muscles.

FYI!

As well as slowing a bike, the rear brake can be used to change the bike's position in mid-air during a jump (see page 32 for more information).

Basic
cornering

> **!** If you remember one thing about turning technique, make it:
> • **Sit down on the seat to lower your center of gravity.**

Flat turns on a motocross track come in all sorts of curves and configurations, but the basic technique for getting around them is pretty much always the same. Turns are another part of riding in which body position plays an important role.

ENTERING THE TURN

Body position is very important when changing direction on your motocross bike. For flat turns you need to lower your center of gravity as much as possible. This means sitting down on the bike's seat when you're finished braking. Slide to the front of the seat as you enter the corner, stick out your inside leg and start to put some pressure on the outside footpeg. Raise your outside elbow and hold your body as close to 90 degrees as possible to the ground while sitting on the outside edge of the seat.

THE MIDWAY POINT

As you reach the **apex** of the turn, steadily start to open the throttle. Keep your body nice and relaxed to help soak up any bumps, but keep the body position described above. Selecting a smooth line through the turn will lessen any chances of the tires losing grip and allow you to keep as much speed as possible.

POWERING AWAY

As you're nearing the exit of the turn you should already be looking forward at the next obstacle. Open the throttle to accelerate away at top speed, and concentrate on applying the acceleration techniques from page 18. Don't forget to put your inside foot back on the footpeg!

apex tightest part of a turn
brake slide skid done deliberately to turn the bike quicker in a corner

SECRET TRICK

Although you should do the majority of your braking before entering a corner, there are times when it's necessary to use the brakes in the turn itself.

1 If you find yourself carrying too much speed through a turn, apply the rear brake slightly. This will stop the front wheel from losing traction.

2 Locking up the rear wheel with the back brake midway through a turn causes the bike to do a small **brake slide**. You can use this to change direction more quickly.

Advanced **cornering**

Once you've mastered the basics of changing direction on your dirt bike, you're ready to learn some advanced cornering techniques. This means it's time to take on ruts **and** berms. **These little channels and dirt banks can make a new rider's life a complete misery.**

RUTS

The key thing to know about ruts is that as soon as your wheels are in one, the rut is in charge of your direction. All you can control is your speed. Relax, ride with the rut and you'll be fine. One common mistake riders make is to look down at their front wheel, then try to steer their way through the rut. This usually leads to the rider overbalancing and crashing. Instead, keep looking forward

BERMS

Berms are less tricky to ride through than rutted turns and can be great places to make up time on the competition. The way to do this is to get your braking done before the turn, line up your wheels, slide your weight forward

SECRET TRICK

Sometimes corner ruts get so deep that your foot controls (the brake pedal on the right or gear lever on the left) dig into them. Chances are you won't notice this happening until your bike mysteriously changes gear by itself, your gear lever gets torn off, or the brake pedal gets bent around so far that you can't use it.

1 When you're racing at a heavily rutted racetrack, adjust the gear and brake levers so they're higher.

2 Most riders move the foot controls so they're higher than the top of the footpeg. This gives more ground clearance and makes it less likely they will get bent or knocked off.

3

rut groove dug out by the passage of bikes, usually found in corners and on the faces of jumps
berm bank of dirt built up on the outside of a corner

at all times. Make sure both wheels are in line as you enter the rut, then follow the normal cornering rules. If you do this properly the rut will guide you around the corner and you'll be accelerating away in no time.

3

4

on the seat, and then lean in with your inside leg forward and your outside elbow high. Just before you get to the apex of the turn

you should be able to open the throttle quite aggressively. The banked side of the berm will allow your tires a little extra grip.

Starts

Motocross races can't be won at the start – but they can definitely be lost. Grab the holeshot and you can control the pace from the front. Get away from the start badly and you'll have to fight your way past a lot of other riders in order to win. Here's everything you need to know about getting off the start line fast.

!
If you remember one thing about starts, make it:
• **Keep your weight forward as you leave the start gate**.

Getting a good start gives you a great chance of winning the whole race.

FYI!
In the days before metal start gates were invented, elastic bungee cords were used to control the start of races.

BODY POSITION
At the start line, sit as far forward on the bike as you can. Have both feet down on the ground, in front of the footpegs. Lean forward with your elbows up and your head over the handlebars. When the 5-second board is turned to signal 5 seconds to go until the start, select second gear, open the throttle about halfway, and feed out the clutch so it's starting to **bite**. Now watch the gate.

bite engage and pull the bike forward
holeshot first place at the first corner of a race
powershift to change up a gear at full throttle and without using the clutch

LEAVING THE LINE

As the starting gate drops, release the clutch and open the throttle fully. The bike will want to wheelie, so keep your weight over the bars to ensure that you keep control. As you power away, move your feet back to the pegs in time for the all-important change into third gear. Move backward in the seat to maximize grip.

MISSION ACCOMPLISHED?

If you've done everything right, you might have your handlebars in front of everyone else's at this point. Your throttle stays fully open as you **powershift** up through the gears on your way to the first turn. Brake as late as you can for the corner, and pick the smoothest line. Make the turn as quickly as possible - you definitely don't want to waste all your hard work and let another racer past.

SECRET TRICK

You might have the best starting technique and fastest bike in the world, but you're not going to take the holeshot if the spot you're starting from isn't properly prepared.

1 All starting gates have a rut in them, worn by the last racer's back wheel. Prepare the rut by kicking it into shape so it's nice and straight. Remove any loose dirt or stones, then stamp down the soil to maximize traction.

2 The photo above shows a well-prepared starting spot on the left, which will give the rider a good start. The rut on the right has been left untouched from the moto before, and will produce a slow start.

Supercross

Big air, killer whoops and bar-to-bar battles – supercross is thrill-a-minute indoor motocross racing. It is rapidly gaining popularity around the world. As a result, there's a pretty good chance that a supercross event will be happening at a stadium near you soon.

EARLY DAYS OF SUPERCROSS

Dirt bikes were first raced inside a stadium in the mid-1950s in Czechoslovakia. However, it was in the United States that supercross first really took off. In the summer of 1972 a race was held in the Los Angeles Coliseum in California. Since then the sport has grown and grown, to the point it now regularly packs out football and baseball stadiums around the world.

AMERICAN MOTORCYCLIST ASSOCIATION SUPERCROSS

The American Motorcyclist Association (AMA) Supercross Championship begins each January and runs until May. This is the biggest supercross race series in the world, and has produced famous riders such as Bob 'Hurricane' Hannah, Jeremy 'Showtime' McGrath and Ricky 'the GOAT' Carmichael. Supercross stars are adored by the public and earn a fortune in prize money and sponsorship deals. The 2007 and 2009 champion James 'Bubba' Stewart even stars in his own reality TV show!

SUPERCROSS AROUND THE WORLD

Supercross is now popular all around the world, particularly in Australia and Europe.

• Australia's national championship series is currently co-promoted by Chad Reed. Reed is a multi-time world, American and Australian supercross champion. The Australian series runs in the later half of the year, and the competition is so good that many American riders use it as a warm-up for the AMA series.

• Europe has many supercross events. Spain, France, Germany and the United Kingdom all have successful championships of their own during the winter months.

There are so many jumps at a supercross race that it sometimes seems the riders spend more time in the air than they do on the track.

FYI!

With 72 victories to his name, Jeremy McGrath has won more supercross events than any other rider in the history of the sport.

Basic jumping

Jumping is a favorite part of motocross for many riders. The good news is that jumping isn't all that difficult. However, it can be very dangerous, so it's important to learn proper techniques and always ride within your limits.

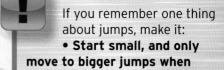

If you remember one thing about jumps, make it:
• **Start small, and only move to bigger jumps when you're 100 percent confident.**

THE APPROACH
Small jumps are perfect for learning how your bike reacts in the air. When learning jump techniques, always start small and work your way up to bigger jumps. When approaching the jump, always make sure you're central on the bike so you're not affecting its overall balance. The faster you hit a jump the higher and farther you go. Always make sure you know what's on the other side of the jump before taking off, and where you want to land.

TAKING OFF
As you ride up the face of the jump, keep the throttle on while maintaining the attack position. As you leave the ramp, slowly ease off the throttle and lean back slightly. This will prevent the rear end of the bike from lifting as the suspension **decompresses**. Stay relaxed and focused.

AIRTIME
Stay central on the bike as you fly through the air, but be ready to lean forward or backward to help keep the bike level. Stay focused on your landing spot, and get ready to return to the ground.

FYI!
In 2008, Ryan Capes did the longest ever jump by a rider on a motocross bike. He jumped 390 feet (118.9 meters).

decompress expand or stretch out
nosedive where the front wheel is too low during a jump

SECRET TRICK

If you find yourself flying through the air with the front wheel lower than the rear, you are in a **nosedive** situation. There are a couple of things you can do to avoid a nasty crash.

1 Pull back on the bars and lean back on the bike. Chances are this won't completely sort out the problem, in which case you will need to try step two.

LANDING

As you come in to land, stay in a central position but be ready to soak up some of the force of the landing with your knees and elbows. Landing with the throttle partially open and the rear wheel driving helps the suspension work properly and softens the impact of landing.

2 Open the throttle quickly in midair. This will increase the speed at which the rear wheel is spinning, which in turn causes it to drop.

Advanced jumping

Complicated jumps such as tabletops **and** doubles **require more skill than small, simple jumps. You have to time the jump so that you land perfectly on the landing ramp, with both wheels hitting the dirt at exactly the same time.**

> **!** If you remember one thing about advanced jumps, make it:
> • **Don't jump tabletops or doubles before you're skilled at changing the angle of the bike in the air.**

FYI!

Advanced jumping techniques were first developed in the mid-1980s by Honda team riders David Bailey and Rick Johnson.

TIMING AND SPEED

To time a jump perfectly, you have to get your approach speed right. This will allow you to jump just the right distance to hit the landing area. Nobody can tell you how fast to go for a particular jump – it's something you learn with time. Build up your experience steadily. Before you try a big, dangerous double, for example, get the technique right on a smaller, simpler tabletop.

APPROACH AND TAKE OFF

Approach the jump in the normal attack position and at the correct speed. As you hit the face of the jump, absorb some of the impact with your knees and elbows, accelerate up the ramp and then slowly turn off the throttle as you leave the ground.

32

SECRET TRICK

What do you do if you're flying through the air with the front wheel way too high? Your initial reaction might be to jump off – but there's actually a top trick that might get you out of trouble.

1 Moving from your central position on the bike, shift your weight forward.

2 As you do this, pull in the clutch and tap the back brake pedal with your foot.

These actions will bring down the front end, allowing you to race on like a motocross hero.

AIRTIME

Adjust the angle of the bike with your body as you take off, remembering that you want to land with both wheels together on the **backside** of the jump. When you leave the ramp, the bike's front wheel will be slightly high. Shifting your weight forward should level it off.

HAPPY LANDINGS

Before you start lowering the front of the bike, ready to land both wheels together on the backside of the jump, make sure you *are* going to land on the backside. If you're too short or too long, you'll need to keep the front end high so that the rear suspension can soak up the force of the landing. If you're heading for the backside, get ready to soak up some of the landing with your knees and elbows. Land with the throttle partially on and power away.

backside downward-sloping landing area of a jump

double pair of jumps positioned so that it's possible to jump from the first and land on the backside of the second

tabletop jump similar to a double but with the gap between the two peaks filled in

33

Extreme conditions

If you remember one thing about riding in extreme conditions, make it:
- **Prepare yourself and your bike well.**

Motocross is already a hazardous and tough sport, but occasionally extreme weather or track conditions make it even harder. The two things you need when this happens are perfect preparation and a positive mental attitude.

MUD

When it's been raining heavily and the track's a muddy mess, don't be dismayed. Prepare yourself and your bike with particular care. Concentrate on taking the lead at the start of the race. If you can manage this you can control the race from the front, and mud from other people's tires won't be sprayed up into your face. A small towel tucked in your pants will allow you to clean your grips and gloves if you do crash.

SAND

Sand races are notoriously tough on your bike and your body. You need to be as fit as possible. Your bike should be prepared as carefully and completely as it can be (see pages 40 and 41). Ride smoothly to keep your overall speed as high as possible at all times. It's likely there will be lots of roost, so pay a bit of extra attention to making sure your goggles are perfectly clean and fit really well.

HEAT

It's always important to stay well hydrated, but take extra care to do this if conditions are hot and humid. You will need to drink more fluid than usual. Keep as cool as possible between motos by hanging out in the shade or inside a vehicle with the air conditioning on a cold setting. Wear lightweight **vented** racewear and wet it down with water before your race so it keeps you cool.

COLD

Thermal underwear will help keep your body warm when racing in freezing temperatures. Big **handguards**, rubber undergloves and waterproof thermal socks will help keep your hands and feet more comfortable.

SECRET TRICK

This trick will help you keep your goggles clean for a longer time in muddy or sandy conditions.

Tape an old goggle lens to the top of your helmet peak to make the visor longer. This clear extension helps deflect roost away from your face and goggles but can still be seen through so it won't affect your vision.

This trick also works well if you find that a low sun is blinding you – in this instance use a tinted lens to act as a sun shield.

handguard plastic shield fitted in front of a motorcycle's hand controls
vented fitted with gaps that allow air to flow through

35

Be a **pro mechanic**

Not everyone in life is cut out to be a pro racer – but there are plenty of other jobs available in motocross. If you're good with tools and know motocross bikes inside and out, maybe you could become a professional mechanic.

FYI!

Top mechanics can strip a motocross bike back to the bare frame in less than 20 minutes.

HELPING OUT FRIENDS

Most pro motocross mechanics start out by helping out a friend at a big event. This offers real excitement when all the mechanic's hard work results in good race results out on the track. Top mechanics help ensure that racers don't suffer **DNF**s. The very best mechanics may be offered jobs on pro teams.

A WEEK IN THE LIFE OF A PRO MECHANIC

Here's a typical pro mechanic's week during the racing season.

Monday morning: the cleanup from yesterday's race starts. There are two bikes to wash off, as well as the team truck and awning.

Tuesday to Friday: these four days pass in a blur of stripping bikes, rebuilding them, testing equipment, making adjustments, and preparing two race bikes for the weekend.

Saturday: this day is spent loading the truck and travelling to the track, then putting the two race bikes through technical control, an official checkover.

Sunday, race day: after the racers complete qualifying rounds, mechanics clean and prepare the bike for the first moto and get it to the start on time. After 'pit boarding' the rider through the moto (using boards to communicate lap times, race position and messages of encouragement) it's immediately time to clean, fix and prepare the bike for moto two. When the racing's done for the day, mechanics load up the truck before heading home.

DNF short for 'did not finish'

Cleaning
your bike

Getting your motocross bike dirty is a lot more fun than washing it off afterwards! Even so, this needs to be done after every ride. Here are some top bike-washing tips that'll stop this chore from becoming too much of a bore.

FYI!
Always use a non-**caustic** detergent that's suitable for use on aluminium, titanium and anodized metals.

PRE-WASH PREP
Put a bung in the exhaust and fit a cover over the airbox to keep water from getting in places where it will cause damage. If you don't have an exhaust bung, a rag or sponge will fill the gap. If you don't have an airbox cover, see the secret trick on page 39. (Always remember to take the bung back out once you've finished cleaning!)

GET THE WORST DIRT OFF
Use a power washer and blast off the worst of the dirt. Find someone to tip the bike over so you can clean underneath the frame rails, engine and suspension linkage. Never spray high-pressure water directly at seals, gaskets, radiators or bearings. Remember to spin the wheels to make sure they're clean from every angle.

GET OUT THE SOAP AND SCRUB
When the bike appears to be dirt-free, spray plenty of detergent all over it. Leave it to soak in for a moment, then start agitating the soapy bubbles with a soft brush or sponge. Pay extra attention to areas where there are stubborn stains.

RINSE THE BIKE
When the detergent has had a chance to work, use the washer again to rinse off all the suds. Make sure the brake discs and pads get an especially good rinse clean, because some detergents affect brake-pad performance. Finally, use a water-dispersing lubricant on bare metals and moving parts to keep them from rusting or seizing up.

caustic able to corrode (eat away) metallic surfaces

SECRET TRICK
If you don't have an airbox cover there's an old trick that will keep your filter dry while you wash your bike.

1 Unbolt your seat and take out your air filter.

2 Fit a polythene carrier bag over your air filter, tucking the handle end of the bag up inside the filter.

3 Put the filter back in place, then tighten up the mounting bolt through the bag until the filter is sealed in place. Now you can wash your bike safely in the knowledge that your filter is fully protected from water and detergent.

Pre-ride **preparations**

To prepare your bike you'll need:
- **Screwdrivers**
- **0.3-in and 0.4-in T-bar socket wrenches**
- **Allen keys**
- **Spoke wrench**
- **Air filter service kit**
- **Chain lube**
- **Grease**

You might be in great physical shape. You may know all the essential riding techniques. There may be an awesome race bike parked in your garage. All this will count for nothing if your bike isn't running well. Here are some essential bike-preparation tips to carry out regularly.

FRONT-TO-BACK SAFETY CHECK
Starting from the front wheel, check that every nut and bolt is tight. Starting at the front and working backward means you can't forget anything. Give each bolt a tweak to check it's tight and if it's not, tighten it up. If you're not sure how tight a bolt should be, consult the workshop manual that came with the bike.

FYI!

Not looking after your bike not only increases your chances of a DNF in a race, it also makes the bike worth much less when you sell it.

AIR FILTER
At least once a week remove the filter, take it off the cage and clean it in **solvent**. Squeeze out all excess solvent and wash the filter in hot soapy water. Hang up the filter to dry in the air. When it's dry, inspect the filter for damage. If it's okay, put the filter in a bag and pour in some filter oil. Work the oil in until the

CHAIN - LUBRICATE AND CHECK

Lubricate your chain with off-road-specific oil. Check chain tension by slipping three fingers between the **swingarm** and chain just to the rear of the chain slipper (the plastic strip on top of the swingarm). The chain should be tight across your fingers. If you can't fit three fingers in the gap, the chain needs to be adjusted.

filter is covered. Squeeze out any excess oil, and replace the filter on the cage. Finally, apply a thin coat of grease to the sealing surface and reinstall the filter on the bike.

SECRET TRICK

Most riders can do basic work on their bikes themselves. Many riders, though, have mechanics do engine part replacement and other more complicated jobs.

1 Use your workshop manual to know when the manufacturer recommends work should be done on the bike. This is usually needed after a set number of hours of use.

2 It's surprisingly difficult to keep an exact track of hours an engine has been used. One way to do this is to fit an **aftermarket** hour meter to your bike. Inexpensive to buy and easy to fit, this small part lets you know exactly how long your engine's been running.

aftermarket replacement or additional part
solvent liquid cleaner that removes dirt
swingarm metal arm connecting the rear wheel to the frame

Troubleshooting

There are many elements to motocross, which is partly why it is one of the toughest sports around. Don't worry if you're struggling to get something perfect, because even the best riders occasionally get things wrong. Here are some problems racers commonly encounter, plus some possible solutions.

PROBLEM 1: STRUGGLING IN RUTS

If you're wobbling around rutted turns you need to relearn these key skills:
- Look to the end of the rut rather than down at your front wheel.
- Slide up to the front of the seat when you enter the corner, with your inside leg out.
- Don't fight the rut – let it guide you and your bike around the turn.
- Put a little weight on the outside footpeg to make sure the tires are biting in.
- Accelerate through the rut once you've ridden past the tightest part of the turn.

PROBLEM 2: SLOW AT STARTS

Slow out of the start? It could be time to check your technique isn't slipping:
- Watch the part of the gate that moves first when the starter drops it.
- Start with both feet down so your body is balanced as you leave the line.
- Feed out the clutch smoothly but quickly.
- Make sure you're opening the throttle fully.
- Adjust your body position so you're getting the maximum possible amount of grip without the front wheel lifting.

PROBLEM 3: DIFFICULTY WITH JUMPS

If you're out of control over jumps try the following:
- If you're struggling with a particular jump, it might just be because you're just not ready for it yet. Go back to practicing your technique on smaller jumps such as small tabletops.
- Ensure you keep a neutral body position on the bike as you approach the jump.
- Make sure your speed is sufficient to clear the gap – once you're off the ground there's nothing you can do to speed up or slow down.
- Be ready to pull in the clutch and tap the back brake to bring the front end down, or open the throttle to bring the rear end down.

PROBLEM 4: SLOW THROUGH BERMS

If you're having trouble making it around banked bends, think about these key points:
• Get your braking done before you enter the corner. If you're coming in too fast, not even perfect turning technique will get you around.
• Line up your wheels as you enter the turn.
• Slide up to the front of the seat and put your inside leg out.
• Turn in hard and commit to the bend.
• Keep looking forward.
• Open the throttle when you're past the tightest part of the bend.
• Accelerate away as quickly as possible.

FYI!

Even pro riders usually have a coach whose job is to help them perfect their technique.

PROBLEM 5: BIKE PROBLEMS

If your bike isn't running well it's normally because it hasn't been properly prepared. Remember these key points about bike preparation.
• Whenever you wash your bike, cover the air filter and put a bung in the exhaust.
• If your air filter is dirty or over-oiled, your engine won't breathe properly. Make sure you service this item correctly at least once a week - more often if you ride in dusty or sandy conditions.
• Nothing ruins a race like having your seat or something else fall off. Check all the bike's bolts are tight by doing regular front-to-back bolt checks.

Technical motocross
language

aerobic with oxygen; aerobic exercise improves the performance of the heart and lungs, which circulate oxygen to the muscles

aftermarket replacement or additional part

amateur person who does an activity without pay

apex tightest part of a turn

attack position optimum riding position when accelerating or approaching obstacles

backside downward-sloping landing area of a jump

berm bank of dirt built up on the outside of a corner

bite engage and pull the bike forward

brake slide skid done deliberately to turn the bike quicker in a corner

caustic able to corrode (eat away) metallic surfaces

complex carbohydrate a food that provides energy and helps digestion, such as brown rice, spinach and potatoes

decompress expand or stretch out

dehydrate lose fluid from the body

DNF short for 'did not finish'

double pair of jumps positioned so that it's possible to jump from the first and land on the backside of the second

four-stroke engine that produces power every two turns of the crankshaft

handguard plastic shield fitted in front of a motorcycle's hand controls

holeshot first place at the first corner of a race

line specific route or direction of travel followed by a bike

locking up skidding

loop out crash caused when the front wheel comes up so high that the rider falls off the back of the bike

moto single round of a motocross event

nosedive situation where the front wheel is too low during a jump

off limits not available for use

powershift to change up a gear at full throttle and without using the clutch

pro professional, a person paid to do an activity

roost dirt, dust and debris thrown up by the wheels of a motocross bike

rut groove dug out by the passage of bikes, usually found in corners and on the faces of jumps

solvent liquid cleaner that removes dirt

sprocket toothed disc on the rear wheel, which connects to the chain

swingarm metal arm connecting the rear wheel to the frame

tabletop jump similar to a double but with the gap between the two peaks filled in

throttle twist grip on the right side of handlebar that controls a motorcycle's acceleration

two-stroke engine that produces power on each turn of the crankshaft

vented fitted with gaps that allow air to flow through

Further information

BOOKS

Pro Motocross & Off-Road Riding Techniques Donnie Bales (Motorbooks, 2004)
The third edition of this book has plenty of top tips and techniques that'll help all riders out on the track.

Dirt Bikes Lori Polydoros (Capstone Press, 2011)
This book discusses the history of dirt bikes, dirt bike design, and the most popular dirt bike competitions.

DVDs

Sometimes it's easier to pick up a technique if you're actually shown how to do it:

Stefan Everts MX Training & Racing Techniques
There are currently two DVDs from Everts – one concentrates on sand-riding techniques and the other on hard-packed soil. If you want to pick up some invaluable tips from a 10-time MX world champion, hunt down a copy of each.

Transworld Motocross: Skills series
Transworld Motocross is the world's biggest selling MX magazine and the Skills set of DVDs is very popular.

WEBSITES

Facthound offers a safe, fun way to find Internet sites related to this book. All of the sites on Facthound have been researched by our staff.

Here's all you do:

Visit *www.facthound.com*

Type in this code: 9781429668866

Motocross timeline

1885
Gottlieb Daimler invents and builds the world's first gas-powered motorcycle in Schorndorf, Germany.

1924
The Southern Scott Scramble – the first-ever official motocross race – is held in Camberley, Surrey, in England. The winner, Arthur Sparks, wins the 50-mile race with a time of two hours, one minute, and 51 seconds.

1947
Holland hosts the first ever *Motocross des Nations*, won by the British team of Bill Nicholson, Bob Ray and Fred Rist.

1952
The *Fédération International de Motocyclisme* (FIM) introduces a European championship for riders with 500cc machines. It is won by Belgium's Victor Leloup.

1956
Eighty thousand excited Czechoslovakians watch the first-ever stadium motocross race, in the Strahov Stadium, Prague. The race is just a small part of the Great Victory Day celebrations but is reported to be a favorite with spectators.

1957
The 500cc European series is upgraded to World Championship status. 'Super-Swede' Bill Nilsson wins the title – a feat he'll repeat in 1960.

1962
Thorsten Hallman – another Swede and the creator of the Thor clothing brand – wins the inaugural 250cc World Championship.

1970
Joel Robert powers to victory in the 250cc championship for Suzuki. It's the first time a Japanese manufacturer wins the world title.

1971
Bruce Brown's documentary *On Any Sunday*, starring Steve McQueen, helps introduce the American public to motocross.

1972
Modern supercross is born when the first Superbowl of Motocross is held in the Los Angeles Coliseum. Around 30,000 race fans witness 16-year-old Yamaha rider Marty Tripes take the overall victory.

1973
Yamaha introduces the revolutionary monoshock system on its 250cc factory bike. The single shock absorber not only works more efficiently, but also saves weight over the traditional twin-shock system.

1974
'Flying Dutchman' Pierre Karsmakers becomes the first ever AMA supercross champion. From its beginning in 1974 the American supercross series grows to the point where it now regularly fills stadiums across America.

1975
A third official world championship motocross category is formed for competitors on 125cc machines. Belgium's Gaston Rahier takes the title in the championship's first year – the first of three world titles he will win.

strokes in a newly formed MXGP class. The 500cc class becomes the 650cc class and mixes 500cc two-strokes with four-stroke machines up to 650cc. The 125cc class is opened up to riders on 250cc four-stroke machines. Belgian riders take all three titles, with Stefan Everts winning the MXGP crown, Joel Smets winning the 650cc class, and Steve Ramon winning the 125cc class.

1981
Team U.S.A. wins the Motocross des Nations by dominating in the deep sands of Lommel, Belgium. The team of Donnie Hansen, Chuck Sun, Danny LaPorte and Johnny O'Mara starts a 13-year win streak for the country - the longest in the history of the event.

1983
Brake technology takes a huge leap forward as Kawasaki releases its production KX250 and KX500 models with a front disc brake. Until this point all bikes had been fitted with drum brakes, which were erratic performers at best - especially in the rain.

1993
After 27 years of two-stroke dominance, Belgium's Jacky Martens wins the 1993 500cc world championship on a bike with a four-stroke engine.

1997
Yamaha enters a high-revving four-stroke race machine into the AMA supercross series and the 500cc world motocross championships. The radical YZ400M is a success and a production version - the YZ400F - is launched for the public one year later.

2003
The FIM allows 450cc four-stroke machines to race against 250cc two-

2004
The world championships receive another revamp. The MXGP class is now known as MX1, the 125 division MX2 and the 650 class MX3.

2006
Two of the greatest racers retire from full-time competition. Belgium's Stefan Everts bows out with 10 world titles and 101 GP wins to his name, while U.S. motocross and supercross sensation Ricky Carmichael ends his career with 16 American national titles and 144 overall wins to his name in AMA competition. Despite being retired, Carmichael notches up another six major wins in 2007 to take his all-time total to 150.

2008
The 2008 model Suzuki RM-Z450 is the first production motocross bike to feature electronic fuel injection. The new system increases power and makes the motor easier to start when stalled. Steve Ramon narrowly misses capturing the MX1 world title on his factory RM-Z450 after a year-long battle with David Philippaerts.

2009
Germany's Ken Roczen becomes the youngest GP winner in motocross history, winning his home round of the world championship at the age of just 15 years and 53 days.

Index